2009

Merry Christmas
to
Rob

From

Mom & Dad

Hope you are better at
Fudge than me!

Mackinac's

Sweet

FUDGE

Souvenir

by
Phil Porter

Fudge
Mackinac's Sweet Souvenir

by Phil Porter

Mackinac State Historic Parks
Mackinac Island, Michigan

© 2001 Mackinac State Historic Parks

ISBN 0-911872-78-7

First Edition
First Printing, 5,000 copies

Art Director: Thomas Kachadurian
Cover photographs: © 2001 Thomas Kachadurian

Foreword

The Mackinac State Historic Parks were created to preserve the historic places and the stories of Michigan's Straits of Mackinac. Using historical collections, archives, archaeology and research, our curators and historians have created one of the foremost history organizations in the nation. At Fort Mackinac, Colonial Michilimackinac, Historic Mill Creek and Mackinac Island State Park, hundreds of thousands of visitors encounter the past in lively exhibits and interactive pro-grams every summer. The programs have earned accreditation by the American Association of Museums and recognition by scholars—but our understanding of history goes well beyond formal studies.

Coming to Mackinac, and understanding its heritage, requires one to experience what life was like, to share traditions and to create memories for future generations. There is no better way to share in the heritage of Mackinac than to sample the foods that made it famous, and no food treat is more memo-rable than Mackinac fudge. Almost everyone who leaves Mackinac takes away a sample of this island staple, made famous since the early 20th century as the island's best souvenir. How did it come to be that way? What changed Mackinac from a fur trading center and fishing outpost to a capital of sweets? Mackinac State Historic Parks Chief Curator Phil Porter brings his 25+ years of study of Mackinac history to bear on these intriguing questions.

Recognition for completion of this book must also be given to renowned photographer Bob Cameron and his daughter, island resident and friend Jane Manoogian. They decided that our fudge research could be a resounding success as a book, and on the porch of Grand Hotel one summer day convinced me that it should go forward. Phil Porter did the work with the help of those acknowledged inside but Bob and Jane encouraged us by their enthusiasm. Mackinac Island State Park Commission Chairman Dennis O. Cawthorne and the park commissioners are unfailing in their support for historical projects such as this. Mackinac State Historic Parks is delighted to add *Fudge, Mackinac's Sweet Souvenir* to the history of this special place.

Carl R. Nold

Director, Mackinac State Historic Parks
Mackinac Island State Park Commission

MACKINAC ISLAND AND FUDGE – the place and the product have been inextricably linked for more than seventy-five years. Along with riding bikes, taking a carriage tour and visiting the fort, buying a box of fudge has been a "must-do" Mackinac Island activity since the Roaring Twenties. The success of this sweet souvenir spawned a multi-million dollar industry housed in more than a dozen quaint fudge shops in the island's small village. Unable to contain such success, the Mackinac fudge phenomenon spread to surrounding Michigan resort communities and to the far corners of the country. Today, "Mackinac Style" fudge is available coast to coast – from Martha's Vineyard to San Francisco's Pier 39 – to satisfy what has become a nation-wide appetite for this tasty treat. Fudge was not invented at Mackinac, but it was here that a particular style of fudge gained great popularity that spread across the nation.

So, to repeat the often-asked question: "Where did this fudge thing come from?" The story begins many decades ago as Mackinac Island was transforming itself from a fur and fish market into a popular summer resort. Shops stocked with merchandise for tourists replaced fur warehouses, cooper shops and fish net stores. Candy makers laid claim to a portion of the tourist market and eventually discovered that the process of making fudge was as important as the sweet product.

Mid-19th century view of the Mackinac Island harbor.

1870s view of Main Street shops selling "Indian Curiosities" and "Confectionery."

Curio Shops and Confections

Mackinac Island began attracting vacationers, health seekers and intellectually curious travelers in the mid-nineteenth century. In response to their arrival, island merchants spruced up their village stores, added new hotels and filled their shelves with souvenirs. There was a particular demand for "Indian curiosities" including cattail reed mats, corn husk dolls, black ash baskets and toy birchbark canoes. By 1847 twenty island merchants maintained "curiosity departments" for visitors who swarmed through the village stores emptying store shelves during the layover of steam boats and sailing vessels passing through the Straits of Mackinac.[1]

Local Indians, particularly the Odawa at nearby L'Arbre Croche, also produced thousands of pounds of maple sugar each year.

Much of this – up to 200,000 pounds a year – was brought to Mackinac Island where it was loaded on steamers and shipped down the lakes.[2] Seeing a potential market among the day visitors, merchants packaged and sold maple sugar in miniature birchbark containers called "mokuks," thus beginning the "confections" business at Mackinac.

The island candy business grew as tourism boomed after the Civil War. War-weary Americans began traveling in great numbers

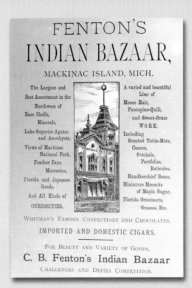

1880s Fenton's Indian Bazaar advertisement featuring "Whitman's Famous Confections and Chocolates."

Indian maple sugar camp by Seth Eastman

and peaceful retreats like Mackinac Island became favored destinations. While Indian items, including maple sugar, remained popular with the new rush of tourists, visitors demanded a wider variety of merchandise including brand-name candies. Island merchants responded by offering "Stuart's Candy" as early as 1868. A few years later "Whitman's Famous Confections and Chocolates" could be found in Fenton's Indian Bazaar between the feather fans and scented table mats.[3]

Packaged candy became a staple item in Mackinac Island curio shop display cases by the late nineteenth century. Many businesses proudly advertised "Confections" on their store awnings and stocked the most up-to-date sweets. Visitors could buy "Lowney's Chocolates" and "Gunther's Superfine Candies" at Bogan's Drug Store. Across the street the Central Drug Store boasted having "Original Allegretti" while Dominick Murray carried A.E. Brooks Candies in his general merchandise store in the Murray Hotel.[4]

The idea of enjoying sweets while on vacation was rapidly becoming part of the Mackinac Island tourist experience, like buying salt water taffy along the boardwalk in Atlantic City, New Jersey. For Victorian-era Mackinac Island travelers, candy was a sweet indulgence, a special treat like visiting Arch Rock, dining on fresh whitefish or shopping for curios. But unlike Arch Rock, whitefish or the locally-made Indian curiosities, these packaged candies had no particular connection to Mackinac. "Lowney's Chocolates" and "Original Allegretti" were no more "local" than the "Lake Superior agates," "Florida ornaments," and "Persian rugs" available on the island's Main Street. The idea of combining the sweet attraction of candy with the allure of local production awaited an adventurous businessman willing to gamble that Mackinac Island would support a full time candy shop providing fresh sweets for daily visitors. In the late 1880s Henry F. Murdick accepted the challenge and opened Mackinac Island's first candy shop.

Murdick Comes to Mackinac

Henry Francis Murdick was born in 1825 in New Haven, Vermont the third of eight children born to Samuel and Betsy Murdick.[5] Following the lead of his father, who left the family during the California gold rush in the 1850s, Henry traveled west to seek his fortune. Trained as a boat builder and sail maker, Henry met and married Sara Jane Leach in Batavia, New York where their son Newton Jerome, nicknamed "Rome," was born in 1866. The

Henry F. Murdick

young family moved to Mt. Clemens, Michigan in 1877 and opened a confectionery. Over the next ten years the Murdicks progressively moved the business north. By 1881 they were in Marine City where "Mrs. Henry Murdick" ran the candy business and six years later they opened a shop in Petoskey, a popular village catering to many nearby summer resorts on Little Traverse Bay.[6] While in Petoskey the Murdicks learned about an even more attractive tourist market – Mackinac Island.

The construction of the magnificent Grand Hotel in 1887 promised to make Mackinac Island the center of upper Great Lakes tourist attention and the perfect spot for a summer candy business. The hotel was built by Petoskey contractor Charles W. Caskey who was known

months with a crew of three hundred men. Family lore suggests that Caskey hired Henry

The first Murdick's Candy Kitchen is the white building on the left in this ca. 1890 view of Main Street.

Grand Hotel, ca. 1890

as a fast builder. He enhanced his reputation when he built the Grand Hotel in less than four

and Rome Murdick to use their sail making skills and equipment to make canvas awnings for the new hotel. Whatever their role in constructing the new hotel may have been, there is no doubt that the construction of the Grand drew the Murdicks to Mackinac Island to open a candy store in 1889.[7]

"Murdick's Candy Kitchen," Mackinac Island's first candy shop, was a modest story-

and-a-half building on the water side of Main Street. Here they made a wide variety of candies to satisfy sweet-toothed summer tourists. Unlike the constant flow of business today, the Murdick's daily boom and bust cycle was created by the great crowds of shoppers who flowed en masse from the large passenger steam boats, swept through the village shops in a buying frenzy and quickly returned before their boats set sail. Murdick's only competition in the early years came from the Chicago Candy Kitchen. Headquartered in Petoskey, the Chicago Candy Kitchen opened a satellite store in "Davis and Son's Old Stand" across the street from Murdick's store in 1899. Billing themselves as the "Sweetest Place in Town," the Chicago Candy Kitchen boasted having the only "up to date candy kitchen in the north" and offered "nice, fresh and clear candies." They also promoted the cleanliness of their shops where visitors could "see it all made"—thus, for the first time, linking

A crude, homemade sign marks the location of the "Chicago Candy Kitchen" next to the Davis Block.

the candy-making process with product sales.

By the mid-1890s Henry was anxious to return to his earlier passion of boat building, a skill that he had shared with his son Rome. With their candy store well established, Henry and Rome launched the "National Park Boat Livery" on the lake side of their candy shop. Here island visitors leased row boats for picnics on Round Island, sailed "cat boats" around the

11

bay or chartered the "sailing yacht" for longer excursions. The Murdicks also sold boats, spruce poles for masts and flag poles. They continued to

Murdick's Boat livery behind the Candy Kitchen, ca. 1900.

operate both businesses for many years.[8]

While Henry focused his efforts on the boat livery, Rome concentrated on running the candy business. It was Rome who first made commercial fudge at Mackinac on marble slabs, a process which gave their product a unique flavor and provided a show for visitors. Rome, like many later fudge makers, was a showman at heart. While making fudge at southeast

Michigan fairs around the turn of the century, he offered a "free ring" with every pound of candy sold. Once the sale was completed, Rome would whirl around and strike a brass bell for the customer.[9] Rome's eldest son Gould, born in 1892, carefully watched his father and quickly learned the recipes and rituals for successful candy sales, skills that he would put to good use many years later.

The Murdick candy business subsided for a while after Henry's death in 1908, but there were others eager to fill the demand for Mackinac-made candy. During the 1910s a "Miss English" had a small candy store on Astor Street across from the City Hall.[10] Her competition included Ferguson's Candy Kitchen on Main Street. In 1912 Alex "Candy" Ferguson offered a "full line of fruits, popcorn, peanuts and 'tailor made' candies as well as salt water candy and Merry Widow kisses."[11] Ferguson installed a large hook on his shop wall for pulling taffy, a candy-making event that was much enjoyed by his customers. Flush with success, Ferguson added a bakery in a new addition that he constructed in 1913. Disaster struck, however, one summer evening when his building caught fire. Ferguson rushed to the store and began throwing equipment, supplies and boxes of candy out of the windows to save what he could. Hearing the city fire bell, local children flocked to the fire and joyfully scooped up the jettisoned boxes of candy

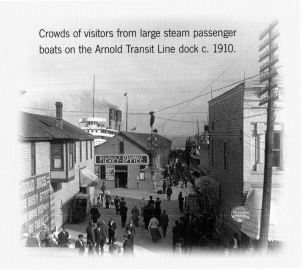

Crowds of visitors from large steam passenger boats on the Arnold Transit Line dock c. 1910.

surrounding the burning building. [12]

In 1914, perhaps to fill the void created by the Ferguson Candy Kitchen fire, Emma Angell and Cora Phelps opened their Mackinac Island candy store. As young friends, Angell and Phelps enjoyed candy making and developed many of their own recipes. At first working out of a single showcase, the young women eventually offered a wide variety of candies including hand dipped chocolates, nut brittles, fragrant mints, pecan pralines and creamy fudge. Well received by Mackinac Island visitors, the women established a more permanent sales location in the Marquette building at the corner of Fort and Main streets. Angell and Phelps remained in the island candy business for the next twenty-eight years and, although they did not put on a show like the bell-ringing Rome Murdick or the taffy-pulling "Candy" Ferguson, the women were always known for their quality candies and tasteful store.[13]

Fudge Comes to the Fore

World War I had a dramatic impact on Mackinac Island's tourist economy, especially the candy makers. As the nation's energy and attention turned to war, summer vacations became an extravagance that most people could not afford. The number of visitors to Mackinac Island took a sharp drop. Sugar rationing and the high price of available sugar provided a further blow to Mackinac candy makers. The sugar not available to island confectioners was used to produce candy for soldiers, a circumstance that eventually would benefit Mackinac Island candy makers.

During World War I millions of individually-wrapped one-ounce portions of chocolate were manufactured and shipped to United States soldiers in Europe. Not surprisingly, soldiers developed a taste for chocolate and the "candy bar" became a dominant confection after the war. Many well-known candy bars were developed in the decade following World War I including the "Baby Ruth," "Butterfinger," and "Oh, Henry."[14] At Mackinac, chocolate-hungry Doughboys enjoying post-war vacations helped revive the island candy business.

Rome Murdick joined forces with his son Gould and reestablished Murdick's Candy Kitchen in the early 1920s.[15] Though seriously injured in the war and suffering with a heart condition and permanent loss of hearing, Gould inherited his father's gift of showmanship and soon developed an enticing menu of activities to draw people into the candy shop. A talented musician, Gould would sit at the store piano "rappin out some tunes" until the room was full of tourists. He would then jump up and sell

Chocolate (with and without nuts) is the most popular fudge flavor. Chocolate is made from the fruit of the cacao tree, a native of Central and South America. Originally consumed as a bitter drink by Mayan and Aztec Indians, chocolate was introduced to Europeans by Columbus, Cortez and other New World explorers. Eventually sweetened and served as a hot drink, chocolate became very popular throughout Europe and colonial America. Chocolate first appears in the Straits of Mackinac as a popular, though pricey, drink enjoyed by eighteenth-century French and British residents at Fort Michilimackinac.

Chocolate manufacturers began producing solid chocolate products in the mid nineteenth century. Today, Mackinac Island fudge makers purchase thousands of pounds of unsweetened chocolate every summer to satisfy their customers' cravings.

Murdick's first candy shop on Mackinac Island's Main Street ca. 1925

to blow the smell of cooking candy into the street. Gould even went so far as to pour vanilla flavoring into a bubbling cauldron of candy. The vanilla instantly dissolved, adding no flavor to the fudge but creating a sweet-smelling aroma that wafted into the street to lure unsuspecting passers-by.

Under Rome's tutelage, Gould learned to make marble slab fudge with dramatic flair. The entire fudge making process was a public event that took place in the back of the store where the candy chefs demonstrated their craft. The ingredients – sugar, butter, cream, corn syrup and flavoring – were mixed in a coke-fired copper kettle and slowly brought up to temperature. Using wooden paddles the candy maker gently stirred the mix until it reached the optimum heat – about 230 degrees depending on barometric pressure, humidity and the temperature of the marble slab. The steaming concoction was poured on to the marble slab and

them all candy. Also an excellent accordion player, Gould understood that entertainment was as essential as sugar to successful candy sales.[16] To further draw people into the store, Rome and Gould used the kitchen-cooling fans kept in place with removable stainless steel bars. Once the mixture begun to cool and stiffen, the candy maker removed the bars and began to work the slowly-stiffening liquid into a creamy solid candy. Here the theatrically-inclined fudge man could really put on a show. He allowed the gooey mass to nearly ooze off the side of the slab. Mesmerized visitors gasped in delight as he swept along the edge with his long-handled trowel and folded the mouth-watering candy back into the center of the table. The candy maker continued to work the candy, making it progressively harder, until he formed the final loaf of fudge with a short scraper. While the fudge was still warm, he sliced half-pound pieces that fit neatly into the "Murdick Candy Kitchen" boxes. Today, the fudge making process is essentially the same, although gas has replaced coke for heating the copper candy kettles.

Murdick's fudge-making process and deli-cious product were huge hits with the swelling crowds of post-war visitors. Murdick made other candies (probably to break the monotony of making fudge all day) but these waxed and waned in popularity. First it was taffy, then a "peanut concoction" became the rage until it was replaced by kisses. Finally, it became apparent that fudge alone was the consistent favorite.[18] Eager to stake a claim to their popular candy, Rome and Gould patented the trademark "Murdick's Famous Fudge" in 1923.

Always aware that the making of the candy was as important as the final product, Gould encouraged island visitors to "Come in and see Murdick make his famous fudge" in local newspaper advertise-ments.[19] To satisfy long distance customers, the Murdicks guaranteed candy ship-ments across the country. This service, now offered by all the island candy mak-ers, accounts for thousands of pounds of fudge being mailed from Mackinac Island every summer.

Murdick's only competition through-out this period came from Angell and Phelps, who sur-vived the war years at Mackinac and were ready to take advantage of the prosperous '20s. In 1922 the women moved from the Marquette building into a store-front on the southwest end of the Chippewa Hotel where they remained for nearly twenty years. Eager to stay away from the flashy fudge business, Angell and Phelps developed a reputation for produc-ing high quality candy in their "spotless kitchens" and selling it in their tastefully decorated store. The women eventu-ally added a line of quality gifts including glassware. They also established a small satellite store in the Arnold Line dock passenger waiting room to give departing visitors one last chance to take home a sou-venir box of Mackinac Island candy.[20]

SUNDAY, JUNE 17, 1934

COME IN AND SEE
MURDICK MAKING HIS FAMOUS FUDGE
He will guarantee shipments anywhere.
MURDICK'S CANDY KITCHEN

ANGELL & PHELPS
Makers of Fine Candies
In Our Own
Spotless Kitchens
•
Mail Orders Carefully
Packed and Shipped

Chippewa Hotel Building
Mackinac Island

Main Street, Mackinac Island, ca. 1920

Sons sold a full line of "Bunte's Candies" in their impressive brick front store. Bunte Brothers, a well-established Chicago candy company, developed a process for putting soft fillings inside hard candies in 1905. The company eventually manufactured more than 500 varieties of suckers and is still in the candy business today.[21] Despite the national popularity of these manufactured candies, it was locally-produced sweets that Mackinac Island visitors wanted to buy. This demand eventually encouraged others to establish candy shops, but they would have to wait until the island weathered the economic storms of the Great Depression and World War II.

Angell and Phelps further expanded their candy empire by opening a shop in Daytona Beach, Florida in 1925. For many years they worked the island tourist business in the summer and the Daytona Beach crowd in winter.

While the Murdick family and Angell and Phelps perfected their candy making skills, other island merchants continued to purchase and sell factory-made candy. By 1920 Bogan's Drug Store proudly offered "Huyler's Candies" for sale to their customers and J. W. Davis and

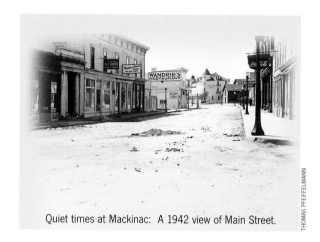

Quiet times at Mackinac: A 1942 view of Main Street.

THOMAS PFEIFFELMANN

Hard Times for Candy Makers

In the summer of 1929 Rome and Gould Murdick moved their candy business into a new store. The prospects for success were excellent. They had a popular and well-established business, tourist traffic was strong and growing and their new location in the center of town was close to the boat docks and right next door to the telegraph office. Their optimism was short lived, however, because of the economic disaster set in motion by the stock market crash that October.

Summer vacations became an unaffordable luxury for most people during the Great Depression and continuing through World War II. Many island businesses were forced to close and others suffered lean years during these hard times. The island candy makers were no exception.

Both the Murdicks and Angell and Phelps struggled through the Depression as many penny-watching tourists resisted their tempting sweets. The Murdicks' problems were further complicated as Rome's health failed and Gould, still suffering from his war wounds, was forced to carry the workload. Candy making, especially the slab fudge process, is strenuous work. Carrying large bags of sugar, lifting heavy candy kettles and bending over and troweling the fudge, all in a hot, steamy environment, took its toll on the candy makers. By 1930 Gould Murdick was anxious to find help and he placed an advertisement for a candy maker in the trade magazine "Confectionery Journal." Harold May, a Kansas-born candy chef looking for summer work, responded to the ad.

May, a second-generation candy maker, had always been able to find work during the winter months. Thanksgiving, Christmas, Valentine's Day, Easter and Mother's Day were excellent candy-selling holidays. By contrast, summers were the "off season" for early twentieth-century confectioners. Murdick's offer provided the thirty-eight-year old May with an

Back to the Future: In the 1930s Ethel May made hand dipped candy in the same kitchen where her granddaughter Tienne was still hand dipping May's candies in the next century.

opportunity to support his young family by making candy in the summer – and at a charming and beautiful resort no less! Armed with his thick book of candy recipes, including twenty-six different types of fudge, May moved to Mackinac Island in the summer of 1930 and became Gould Murdick's chief candy chef. The Mays – Harold, his wife Ethel, an excellent chocolate dipper, and their three-year old son Marvin – moved into two rooms above Murdick's Main Street store and began a candy making career that would continue for several generations.[22]

Harold May worked summers at Murdick's Candy Kitchen during the Depression and war years. Business was strong enough to keep the shop open, but profits were slim and May and his fami-ly had to find winter work each year which took them to candy shops around the country. It was during these winter jobs that his son Marvin began to work at his side and learn the trade.[23] Each summer the Mays returned to Mackinac and helped Gould keep the business going during those lean years, especially after Rome's death in 1935. Other island candy makers were not so fortunate.

Heppe's Candy Store was a short-lived victim of the slow economy. Harry Heppe opened his first candy store in Philadelphia in the 1880s. His sons Leroy and Harry L. continued and expanded the business to include a chain of stores along the East Coast and in Florida. Envisioning success at Mackinac Island, the brothers opened a

PURE CANDY IS
VALUABLE FOOD!
Visit
HEPPE BROS.
Originators of
SOUVENIR CANDY NOVELTIES
Makers of Quality Confections
for over 50 years!
Delicious Salt Water
TAFFY
LB. 35¢   3 Lbs. $1.00
Home Made Nut Fudge
40¢ Lb.
Parcel Post Shipments Guaranteed
—: Send Some Home :—
HEPPE BROS.
Murray Bldg.   Mackinac Island

store in the Murray Hotel in the summer of 1940. Heppe's customers purchased salt water taffy for 35¢ a pound and "home made nut fudge" for a nickel more.[24] But Heppe's specialty was candy novelties including sweets made in the form of fruits such as apples, oranges and strawberries, brown crusty looking candy "pork chops" and candy "foaming beer mugs" filled with honey taffy and topped with a "froth of delicious nougat."[25] These unique confections offered little competition to Murdick's "famous fudge" and Heppe's closed for good at the end of their first summer.

After twenty-seven consecutive years in the Mackinac Island candy business, Angell and Phelps closed their Chippewa Hotel store at the end of the 1940 season. The women moved permanently to Florida and focused their energy and resources on keeping the Daytona Beach store open. Their hard work paid off and the Florida store still operates today under the

This Chippewa Hotel store front was home to three different candy makers: Angell and Phelps, Verna Murdick and Selma Dufina.

same name but with new owners. Gould Murdick purchased Angell and Phelps' candy making equipment and in 1941 his wife Verna, also an accomplished candy chef, opened "Verna Murdick's Candy Shop" in the same Chippewa Hotel location.[26] Like Heppe's, Verna's candy shop could not overcome the economic conditions of the early 1940s and closed during the early years of World War II as sugar rationing was imposed.

Rationing had a profound impact on

A crowd of tourists line up to purchase fudge from Harold May during World War II when sugar was rationed and candy sales were limited to a few hours a day.

Mackinac Island during World War II. By 1943 restrictions on the sale of rubber tires, automobiles and gasoline reduced the island's summer tourist business to a trickle. Most businesses that survived the economic impact stayed open all day to take advantage of every potential customer. Murdick's Candy Kitchen, now the island's only candy shop, was a unique exception because the sugar ration severely reduced their capacity to make candy. Although candy chef Harold May could easily have made and sold their allotment of candy by the end of June, he preferred to stay open all summer by selling smaller amounts each day. Every morning while the doors were still locked, May made the day's batch of candy and fudge. In early afternoon he opened the doors, often to a long line of waiting customers, and sold out his inventory, limiting each customer to no more than one pound of fudge.[27] Murdick's continued to operate on this part-time basis throughout the war because their quota of sugar never increased.

By the mid 1940s Gould Murdick was tired of struggling to keep the candy kitchen going. Eager to retire, he sold the business to his long-time loyal employees, Harold and Ethel May, and agreed to stay out of business on the island for at least ten years. Harold changed the store name to "May's Candy Shop" and, even though he was offered the "Murdick's Famous Fudge" banner, he chose "Famous Mackinac Fudge" as his trademark.[28] Harold's purchase was well timed. As the war came to an end, May's Candy shop was the island's lone confectionery, poised to serve the booming post-war crowds who had a pent up desire to travel, sightsee and buy fudge.

Post-War Revival and Expansion

Mackinac Island rebounded as a popular tourist destination after World War II. Americans were ready for a vacation and eager to forget the hardships caused by the war. A vigorous economy allowed people to resume the tradition of summer vacations and an expanding highway system made it easier for them to travel to the Straits of Mackinac. With tires, gasoline and automobiles now available,

Candy makers at work at May's Fudge Shop ca. 1960.

MARVIN MAY

the soldiers' daily rations. Rather then being a once-in-while treat, candy became a daily habit that continued when soldiers came home.[29] The American candy industry boomed after the war and the effect was felt all the way to Mackinac Island.

After years of sugar rationing and belt-tightening ways, Harold May was eager to provide sweets for post-war travelers. Open all day and armed with a storeroom full of sugar, May produced a wide variety of mouth-watering candies. With the help of his son Marvin, Harold made chocolate, maple and vanilla fudge, peanut brittle and pecan glace on the marble slabs. Ethel created chocolate-dipped peanut, cashew, raisin and coconut clusters in the store's small refrigerated room.[30] Fudge continued to be the most popular product, but May's quality chocolates and candies also were well received. The island's fudge reputation spread and growing crowds of summer visitors looked

tourists flocked north to Mackinac. The end of sugar rationing meant that island candy makers could once again provide unlimited supplies of candy and fudge to arriving hordes of visitors, including recently discharged G.I.s.

American soldiers developed an unprecedented taste for candy during the war. Chocolate bars, small, easy to transport and full of energy-producing sugar, were a staple item in for Mackinac-made fudge when they arrived on the island. With a market once again able to support multiple candy stores others soon entered the lucrative business.

Selma Dufina opened Mackinac Island's first new candy store after World War II. Dufina first came to the island in 1928 as a 19-year old student majoring in Home Economics at Michigan Normal College (now Eastern Michigan University). Candy making had been a childhood hobby that Dufina continued after she moved to the island.[31] Dufina became the third Chippewa Hotel candy shop owner when she opened her first store – Selma's Home Made Candy – at that location in 1948. She moved to the Murray Hotel in 1949 and soon established a reputation as an excellent candy maker known for using good ingredients and producing "nice quality candy."[32] Like Angell and Phelps, Dufina eschewed the showier elements of fudge making, and always made her

Selma Dufina's third location was in this candy shop built at the head of the Arnold Transit Line dock in 1962.

candies and fudge in the back room.

Jim Marshall entered the candy business when he opened Marshall's Driftwood Fudge in 1952. Marshall, the great-grandson of Fort Mackinac's longest serving soldier, Ordnance Sergeant William Marshall, learned the candy making trade from the Murdick family. After trying his hand at carpentry, painting and working on Great Lakes freighters, Marshall opened his first shop in the front corner of Ty's

ABOVE: Jerold Murdick (left, cutting fudge) and his son Francis (far right) joined forces with Jim Marshall (second from right) to make fudge at the Michigan State Fair in the early 1950s. RIGHT: Jerold Murdick (left) and son Francis making fudge at the state fairgrounds ca. 1952.

Restaurant on the island's Main Street. Jim made four flavors of fudge – chocolate, vanilla, rum and maple, all with nuts. The cost was $1.00 per pound. Two years later Marshall moved to the north side of the Straits of Mackinac and opened the first fudge shop in St. Ignace.[33] Renamed "Marshall's Mackinac Trail Fudge," the business flourished as the construction of the Mackinac Bridge brought huge crowds of tourists into the area beginning in 1957.

Soon after Marshall left for St. Ignace the Murdick family made its third venture into the island candy business. Jerome Murdick, Gould's half brother, ran Murdick's Luncheonette in the 1940s and early 1950s. In 1956, when Gould's 10-year agreement with May to keep the Murdick family out of the fudge business ended, Jerome eagerly converted his restaurant into a candy shop. Jerome kept the original name – Murdick's Candy Kitchen – but Gould had given the trademark "Murdick's Famous Fudge" to Jerold, another half brother, who opened a Murdick's fudge store in Charlevoix in the early 1950s.[34] Jerome's son Douglas, who learned the finer points of candy-making from Gould, opened the Doug Murdick's Fudge stores in Traverse City in 1964.

FRANCIS MURDICK

Jerold Murdick honed his fudge-making skills at state and local festivals and fairs with his son Francis beginning in the late 1940s. The success of their first state fair in 1948 surprised and delighted the Murdicks. They made fudge for ten days during the fair but never had a chance to put any in the display case because it sold so fast. "We had a tiger by the tail," recalled Francis, who sold fudge from the slab as quickly as he could make it. For eleven years the Murdicks successfully worked a variety of off-season, off-island venues including fairs, boat shows, car shows and festivals.[35] They not only made an excellent profit, they also helped spread the name "Mackinac Fudge" throughout the Midwest. It was at one of these early shows that Jerold and Francis first met Harry Ryba, a young Detroit confectioner who showed great interest in learning more about the fudge business.

Ryba Arrives

Harry Ryba opened his first Mackinac Island fudge store in 1960. Ryba joined May's, Selma's and Murdick's on the island's increasingly-popular Main Street, but he hardly blended into the scene. Within a few years the diminutive, ambitious candy maker created an enormous ruckus with his innovative marketing ideas and clever schemes to grab a piece of the lucrative fudge business. Although Mackinac

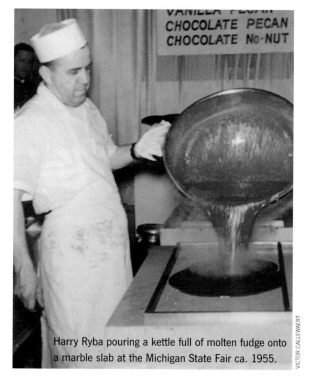

Harry Ryba pouring a kettle full of molten fudge onto a marble slab at the Michigan State Fair ca. 1955.

VICTOR CALLEWAERT

Island had a well-established reputation for producing quality fudge, it was Ryba who spurred the industry to new heights and created an indelible link between "Mackinac" and "Fudge."

Harry Ryba was born in Detroit in 1907 and raised on his parents' farm in Utica, Michigan.

The eldest of five children, Ryba left school after the eighth grade to work on the farm. In the early 1930s Ryba returned to Detroit and worked for Fairmont Creamery selling and delivering dairy products. One of the shops on his route was Harry Coil's Karmel Korn Shop at Chalmers and East Jefferson. In 1936, after Coil was injured in a bicycle accident, Ryba bought the shop and began a career in the confection business.[36]

Ryba made and sold "pan made" fudge until he met Jerold Murdick at one of the state fairs in the late 1940s. The two joined forces and Murdick was soon making Mackinac Island style fudge on his marble slab in Ryba's Karmel Korn Shop. A few years later Francis Murdick replaced his father when Jerold moved to Charlevoix. Ryba carefully watched the Murdick's ply their trade and quickly learned their recipes and successful fudge making techniques. When Francis was sick and unable to come to work one day, Ryba took his place at the copper kettle and made his first batch of Mackinac Island fudge. It was a defining moment in Ryba's career. The energetic, visionary

candy maker had a sense that fudge would be his ticket to a bright future and potential fortune.[37]

Ryba made and sold "Famous Mackinac Island Fudge" in his Detroit store for nearly a decade before he established a shop on the island. When Phil Corby's Main Street fudge store became available in 1960, Ryba jumped at the chance to get a foothold in the profitable Mackinac Island market. With help from his partner and son-in-law Victor Callewaert, Ryba was soon in business and looking for ways to boost sales. His successful tactics were reminiscent of those used 50 years earlier by the bell-ringing showman Rome Murdick.

Like his predecessors, Ryba knew that the process of making fudge, the "action" as he liked to call it, was essential for successful sales. While other fudge shops were content to demonstrate candy making in the back of their stores, Ryba moved the process to the front window. Throngs of tourists walking along Main Street crowded in front of Ryba's to watch his candy makers dramatically ply their trade. Ryba further enticed the gawking crowd by using the old Murdick ploy of blowing the sweet smell of fresh candy out the front door. Over the years all the island candy makers have capitalized on this idea, some have even installed intake fans over the fudge slabs and vented them through the eaves above the sidewalks.

Ryba aggressively looked for other methods of spurring sales. He used radio commercials and billboards to push his product. He experimented with new recipes and by 1965 boasted ten flavors of fudge, twice as many as his competition. He priced his fudge a nickel higher than the others (a whopping $1.25 per pound!) to create the illusion that his was the "premium" product. For those willing to make a bigger investment, Ryba offered a lifetime supply of fudge, at the rate of three pounds per month, to customers willing to pay $2,250 in advance. The "lifetime," he added, "being yours or mine, whichever ends sooner."[38] Ryba packaged his fudge in bright pink boxes, a colorful alternative to the traditional white ones used by the other candy makers.[39] His customers also were given matching shopping bags with handles for carrying their fudge and other purchases. Although this was an added expense, Ryba knew that each bright pink "Ryba" bag on the arm of a Main Street tourist provided excellent advertising.

Ryba's competitors, who had been content to produce quality candy and reap a reasonable profit, bristled at the newcomer's aggressive, competitive style, especially when he took the moniker "Mackinac's Fudge King." A verbal war with charges and counter-charges flew between island candy makers. Claiming that Ryba was

Capitalizing on Mackinac's sweet souvenir, ice cream makers began producing "Ryba's Mackinac Island Fudge" ice cream in the mid 1980s.

the source of the problem, Selma Dufina told the Detroit Free Press, "Since he came here, it's been a vicious circle around here. The only thing we don't do these days is throw fudge at each other."[40] Marvin May leveled the more serious charge of copyright infringement, arguing that Ryba's "Famous Mackinac Island Fudge" infringed on May's "Famous Mackinac Fudge." May won his lawsuit, but his unfazed competitor simply took the name "Ryba's Fudge."[41]

All of this controversy played right into Ryba's hand. He loved the publicity and, along with his rivals, enjoyed the increasing popularity of their unique, tasty and now controversial product. As tourist traffic to the island increased in the 1960s so too did the number of fudge stores. Even this didn't bother Ryba, who went so far as to encourage Mary Couls and Florian Czarnecki to open Mary's Fudge Shop in 1962. "The more fudge shops," Ryba explained, "the more we all sell; its mass psychology."[42]

Try Your Own Slab Fudge

Although each candy maker has his own special formula and process for making fudge, the basic recipe hasn't changed much since Henry and Rome Murdick made their first batch of marble slab fudge in the 1880s. Here is a generic recipe for a 35-pound batch of chocolate fudge.

23	lbs.	**sugar**
3.5	lbs.	**corn syrup**
16	oz.	**shortening**
2	tbs.	**salt**
2.5	lbs.	**unsweetend chocolate**
5	quarts	**half and half cream**

Cook to about 232 degrees, cool on the marble slab to 98 degrees and work by hand for approximately eight minutes.

Mackinac Fudge Today and Tomorrow

Ryba's words were prophetic. The island fudge business experienced unprecedented growth in the 1960s and 70s and everyone benefited. Selma Dufina built an attractive new candy shop at the head of the Arnold Line dock in the midst of the "fudge war" in 1962. When Selma retired in 1978 she sold to Kilwin's, a franchise candy business with central offices in Petoskey. Ray Summerfield, a local builder, jumped into the candy business in 1967 when he opened Suzan's Fudge. Two years later he sold to Frank Nephew who renamed the shop "Joann's Fudge" after his wife. Actually, her name is Joan but, typical of the market-conscious fudge makers, Nephew reasoned that the

Presidential Fudge

President and Mrs. Gerald R. Ford enjoyed a two-day visit to Mackinac Island in July 1975. After attending service at Trinity Episcopal Church, the President walked downtown to buy a box of fudge. With little time to prepare, Ford's security staff chose May's Fudge at the corner of Main and Astor streets as the safest venue for the President's buying trip. After tasting a sample of candy maker Ken Kelly's vanilla pecan fudge "fresh off the slab," the President made his purchase with a crowd of curious tourists watching through the windows. Elated with his good fortune, shop owner Marvin May soon proudly displayed a sign reading, "On July 13, 1975, Gerald R. Ford, President of the United States, bought fudge here."

two-syllable sound of "Joann's" had a nicer ring to it. Nephew's friend and business partner Robert Benser bought Murdick's Fudge in 1967 from Jerome Murdick and kept the name while expanding the business. The Murray Hotel even ventured into the candy business, producing oven-cooked "pan fudge" and selling it from their front porch. Over the years all of the island candy makers have opened multiple locations, both off and on the island, in order to provide "fudgies" with ample opportunities to buy their wares.

The popularity of fudge with Mackinac Island visitors resulted in the nickname "fudgie" first appearing in the early 1960s. Ryba laid claim to coining the name. Whether or not it was his invention, the feisty candy maker certainly cemented the relationship between Mackinac and fudge. Eager to capitalize on the new nickname, Ryba began giving away pink "Ryba's Mackinac Island Fudgie" pins with every purchase. Today the term has spread far beyond Mackinac Island

and "fudgie" has become synonymous with "tourist" in northern Michigan and other parts of the country. At the beginning of the new millenium there is no sign that Mackinac Island fudge is waning in popularity. The five marble-

slab fudge makers – May's, Murdick's, Ryba's, Joann's and Kilwin's – now operate fifteen stores on the island which generate millions of dollars in sales every year. Candy makers continue to experiment with new products, perhaps looking for the next candy sensation, or maybe just to break up the monotony of making so much fudge. But at the end of the day it is fudge – creamy, rich and manufactured with dramatic flair – that continues to be Mackinac Island's number one sweet souvenir.

Acknowledgements

This book would not have been possible without the generous advice, assistance and guidance of many individuals. The author especially acknowledges the contributions of:

Jerry MacKenzie

Francis Murdick

Dean Scheerens

Cecelia Flanagan

Marvin May (May's Famous Mackinac Fudge)

Frank Nephew, Armin Porter and Franklin Lambert (Joann's Fudge)

Ronald Steensma (Murdick's Fudge)

Victor and Todd Callewaert (Ryba's Fudge)

Jason Berakovich (Kilwin's Candies)

Wesley Maurer, Jr., St. Ignace News

Notes

1 "Two Days at Mackinac—No. 2," *Democratic Free Press*, (Detroit), 29 July 1847

2 "Two Days at Mackinac-No. 4," *Democratic Free Press*, (Detroit), 31 July 1847

3 *Putnam's Magazine*, New York: G.P. Putnam and Son. Second Volume, July-December, 1868. Dwight H. Kelton, *Annals of Fort Mackinac*, (Chicago: Fergus Printing Company, 1882), 120.

4 Information about late nineteenth-century packaged candy comes from historic photographs and advertisements in period Mackinac Island guide books.

5 Francis Murdick, Interview by author, Mackinaw City, Mich. 30 June 2000; Jerry MacKenzie, Interview by author, Mackinaw City, Mich., 31 July 2000, Mackinac State Historic Parks archives.

6 *Michigan State Gazetteer and Business Directory*, 1887, 1879, 1881, 1883, 1885, 1887-88, Michigan State Library, Lansing, MI.

7 Ibid, 1889.

8 Ibid, 1895-96, 1897, 1899.

9 MacKenzie, interview.

10 Cecilia Flanagan, Interview by author, Mackinac Island, Mich, 14 July 2000.

11 *Republican News* (St. Ignace), 1 June 1912.

12 Flanagan, interview.

13 *Mackinac Island News*, 17 August 1940; Republican News,(St. Ignace) 11 June 1921.

14 Joel Blen Brenner, *The Emperors of Chocolate, Inside the Secret World of Hershey and Mars* (New York: Random House, 1999) 169-70.

15 Otto V. Lang, Interview by Mackinac Island State Park Commission, 1975, Mackinac State Historic Park Archives.

16 MacKenzie, interview.

17 Murdick, interview.

18 *Mackinac Island News*, Saturday 9 August 1941.

19 *Mackinac Island News*, 17 June 1934.

20 Lang, interview.

21 Brenner, 168.

22 Marvin May, Interview by author, Mackinac Island, Mich. 28 October 1998.

23 Ibid.

24 *Mackinac Island News*, 20 July1940.

25 Ibid.

26 *Mackinac Island News*, Saturday 9 August 1941.

27 May, interview.

28 Ibid.

29 Brenner, 171.

30 May, interview.

31 W. T. Rabe, "O! Fudge!" [n.d., ca. 1980] Mackinac Island State Park Commission Archive.

32 May, interview.

33 "About Marshall's" [company history], Marshall Fudge and Candy Company [web site], Retrieved 2000. Available from www.marshallsfudge.com.

34 Arletta Murdick MacKenzie, "Murdick's Famous Mackinac Island Fudge – A Centennial Confection." [n.d. ca. 1987] Mackinac State Historic Parks Archives.

35 Murdick, interview.

36 *The Sacramento(California) Bee*, 10 March 1996, section B, p 7; Rabe, "O! Fudge!"

37 Rabe, "O! Fudge!"; MacKenzie, interview; Elizabeth Edwards "The Fudge Factor, ", *Traverse* (August 1998): 76.

38 *The Sacramento(California) Bee*, 10 March 1996, section B, p 7.

39 David C. Smith, "Squaring Off Over Chocolate Squares: Mackinac's Great Fudge War", *Detroit Free Press*, 19 September 1965.

40 Ibid.

41 Ibid; Edwards, "The Fudge Factor," *Traverse* (August 1998): 76.

42 David C. Smith, "Squaring Off Over Chocolate Squares: Mackinac's Great Fudge War", *Detroit Free Press*, 19 September 1965.